RISEN: THE STORY OF THE RESURRECTION

WRITTEN BY PAUL A. LYNCH

Table of Contents

Introduction

All our hope is in God. This is what the Holy Bible teaches us. Outside of God, we cannot survive; there is no alternative worth considering. Everything is in God's hands. All things were created by Him, through Him, and for His purpose (see Colossians 1:16–20). We are also reminded that all things work together for good for those who love God (see Romans 8:28).

Although we may now boldly say that we love God, that we live by grace, are freed from sin, and are on our way to heaven, all of this would be meaningless if Christ had not died and risen from the dead. Without His resurrection, life on earth would be empty and filled with despair. The most significant power in both the visible and invisible realms is the power of the resurrection. This scripture reminds us of Romans 6:1.

Romans 6:1

"What shall we say then? Shall we continue in sin, that grace may abound?"

This book is a brief account that analyses and tells the story of the resurrection of Jesus Christ.

The Upper Room

The Jewish Passover is called **Pesach**. Its purpose is to commemorate the enslavement of the Jewish people in Egypt and how God delivered His people by judging the Egyptians and setting the Hebrews free. It was a system of oppression and bondage. Slavery, however, is not a new phenomenon; it has existed since the earliest times.

Jesus taught that people are slaves to whatever they obey (see Romans 6:16). If we obey sin, we become slaves to sin; if we obey righteousness, we become slaves to righteousness. This truth reminds us why the Hebrews found themselves in slavery in Egypt in the first place.

Joseph rose to become a great ruler under Pharaoh after interpreting the Pharaoh's dreams. He was one of Jacob's sons, who later received the name Israel from the Angel of the Lord. Joseph was the son of Rachel, and his father favoured him, giving him a coat of many colours. This caused his brothers to envy him greatly.

Joseph was a dreamer, and whenever he had a dream, he shared it with his family. Each revelation increased his brothers' jealousy, while his father, Israel, reflected on what Joseph had said.

His brothers kidnapped him and sold him to his cousins, the Ishmaelites. The Ismaelites were descended from Ismael. Ismael was the one who begot the Arab nation. The Arab nation today comprises the Islamic peoples of the Middle East and their descendants.

Joseph was sold by the Ismaelites to the Egyptians. An Egyptian high official called Potiphar bought him, and he found favour with Joseph. In time, Joseph became the household leader until Potiphar's wife tried to seduce him. She enticed Joseph every day. Joseph refused. He saw this as wickedness in the eyes of God. There were no "Ten Commandments" yet, but he knew the concept of sin. The wife lied about Joseph, and her husband tossed him into prison. Potiphar knew he was innocent. At the time, the Hebrew boy was young, in his early twenties. In prison, he got the breakthrough. He became the leader of the other prisoners. This didn't happen overnight. Often, we believe that when we pray, everything should change immediately. However, the Bible tells us otherwise. It tells us everything happens in its own time (Ecclesiastes 3:1).

A few years later, he saw two prisoners, a butler and a baker. These men had worked for Pharaoh in the past. Both offended him and were thrown into prison. Defying Pharaoh could bring forth death. Both men fell asleep that night and had a dream. One dreamt he was pouring wine in Pharaoh's cup, and the other saw that birds ate cakes from a basket in his hands. Both men woke up sad. The Bible provides insight into this in the Book of Genesis, as dreams were important in Ancient Egypt. In the dynasty, many magicians, soothsayers, and astrologers worked for Pharaoh.

Joseph saw the butler and baker, and saw the sad look on their faces. Being the type of man that he was, he asked them why they looked miserable. They explained that they had dreams that needed an interpreter. Joseph heard the dreams and interpreted them. He told the butler he would serve wine as before in three days, and the chief baker would be hanged in three days. In three days, everything he had told them was fulfilled. However, Joseph had to wait several years because, although he told the butler to remember him before Pharaoh, he somehow didn't until the king had two dreams. Now was the time that God was about to bring him out of prison and into a palace. Pharaoh dreamed, and he saw seven fat cows and seven skinny cows grazing on the banks of the River Nile. And he noticed that the seven ugly, skinny-looking cows ate the fat ones and still looked the same.

He also had another dream in which he saw seven ears of corn battered by the east wind, and they remained the same. With all these dreams, he knew something was up. He called for all the magicians, soothsayers, and astrologers in his kingdom, but none could interpret the dreams. He called upon the gods of Egypt, but none could help.

His butler noticed the sad look on his face, and he remembered Joseph the Hebrew, who was in prison. He explained to Pharaoh, and he sent for him. Joseph interpreted the dreams, and the king was amazed that someone like him had lived on earth, with the Spirit of God within him.

Genesis 41:38

"And Pharaoh said unto his servants, Can we find such a one as this is, a man in whom the Spirit of God is?"

Joseph was promoted because he interpreted the Pharaoh's dreams. Several months later, Israel or Jacob sent his sons into Egypt to buy food. By this time, they had forgotten Joseph because the sons of Israel told their father for many years that he was dead. The sons of Israel had to bow down before Joseph in Egypt. Joseph's dreams that he'd gotten earlier were fulfilled. All his siblings and parents bowed before him in honour and reverence. This took place in Egypt. Joseph became the hero who saved millions of lives from starvation and famine. Joseph himself said that everything his brothers did and thought was evil was working for the good.

Genesis 50:20

"But as for you, ye thought evil against me; but God meant it unto good, to bring to pass, as it is this day, to save much people alive."

Fast forward a few years, and the Bible in Genesis states that a pharaoh in Egypt became king and didn't know about Joseph. From a logical point of view, this seems odd. For example, a new president, king, queen, or prime minister rose to power in your country, but they don't know who the previous king, prime minister, or president was. This is what the Bible mentioned. Because of this lack of historical knowledge about the Pharaoh, the Hebrews were imprisoned and forced to work in the mud. This period isn't mentioned. It could be less than 100 years or more than 100 years. The truth is, neither the Bible nor the historical story gives us that information. Let's not speculate.

The Hebrews, or children of Israel, spent over 400 years as enslaved people in Ancient Egypt, working in the mud, serving the Egyptians, and working on pyramids. This action grieved the people, and they cried out to God, who heard them. God himself remembered his covenant or promises he'd made with the patriarchs Abraham, Isaac, and Jacob. This is the Abrahamic covenant mentioned in Genesis chapters 12 and 17.

God will give Abraham's descendants a land flowing with milk and honey. Another aspect is that God will bless those who bless Israel and curse those who curse Israel. The children of promise will be blessed forever by the Lord God who created heaven and earth.

God took up Moses, the prince of Egypt, to prepare his people for this blessing. This is recorded in Exodus 3. Moses became a murderer, fled from the pharaoh into Midian, and became a shepherd. He also married one of Midian's daughters. God sent Moses and Aaron to set the people free. Ten plagues were sent to Egypt, and the tenth and final was the most deadly. That's the killing of the firstborn of the Egyptians.

Blood on the Doorposts

God commanded Moses to tell the people to kill a lamb without blemish, wrinkle, or spot and place its blood on their doorposts, because in the night the angel of death would pass over Egypt. All the people who did this were spared from the pestilence that walked in darkness and the noisome demon. The firstborn sons of the Egyptians were destroyed. Pharaoh saw this and finally decided to let God's people go. However, that was quickly withdrawn when he decided to send his army after the Hebrews. The Egyptian armies were finally destroyed in the Reed Sea or the Red Sea.

The blood of the lamb on the doorposts represented the blood of Jesus Christ. As recorded in scripture, it was a shadow of the good things to come in Christ. Without the shedding of blood, there is no remission of sins (Hebrews 9:22).

Only the blood of Jesus Christ washes away sins. At the same time, the angel of death patrolled the streets and corners of Egypt while the Hebrews ate the Pesach or Passover. They commemorated and reflected on their existence as a people who were once enslaved people in the country of Egypt for generations.

There's also a particular reason why the Hebrews became enslaved. For one, the money had failed in Egypt. In other words, money became useless because people wanted food, and money couldn't be eaten. The other reason was that the people of God became comfortable in Egypt. Egypt in the Bible is a rich country that many people have travelled to. Even Jesus Christ travelled to Egypt because his life was at risk as a baby. He stayed there until Herod was dead.

Egypt was a superpower in biblical times, but it also represented bondage. The material wealth in Egypt could blind the eyes of those who weren't spiritually watchful. Babylon, Egypt, Sodom, and Gomorrah, the city of the Philistines, and some other places all represented bondage in the spiritual sense. As long as God lived, the Hebrews couldn't stay in Egypt or any other strange land. The Hebrews had to go into the land that was promised to them. This story of the firstborn is literal, according to the Holy Bible. It's also symbolic of the power that we'd have in Christ.

The Upper Room- A Place of Power

The upper room is a place of power. It's also a place where Christ ate the Passover with his disciples. This

Passover, Christ changed to the Lord's Supper. Passover is different from the Lord's Supper. The wine represented the New Testament in his blood. And the unleavened bread represented his body that was broken for us. There's no longer bitter herbs, lettuce, apple, nor honey, but it's a new thing in Christ Jesus the Lord. The Passover no longer represented bondage in Egypt, but now it represents the power we have in Christ and freedom from the law of sin and death. Christ came and fulfilled the Law. Remember, the Law was a shadow of the good things to come in Christ. It was a type and shadow of those things which were set up long ago. Which is greater: the shadow, the type, or the actual thing? We'd all agree the "actual thing" is better than both type and shadow. For example, the Temple in the Old Testament represented Christ, his body, and holiness. God's presence didn't dwell in the physical temple, but rather it dwelt in His people and prophets. King Solomon considered building a temple for God to live in because, in his mind, God's glory was magnificent. If God's so great, why not make a temple to contain His glory? In the next chapter, we see that King Solomon came to his senses and realised that Heaven and Earth itself can't contain the glory of God (see 1 Kings 8).

Luke 22:14-20

English Standard Version

Institution of the Lord's Supper

14 And when the hour came, he reclined at table and the apostles with him.

15 And he said to them, "I have earnestly desired to eat this Passover with you before I suffer.

16 For I tell you I will not eat it until it is fulfilled in the kingdom of God."

17 And he took a cup, and when he had given thanks he said, "Take this and divide it among yourselves.

18 For I tell you that from now on I will not drink of the fruit of the vine until the kingdom of God comes."

19 And he took bread, and when he had given thanks, he broke it and gave it to them, saying, "This is my body, which is given for you. Do this in remembrance of me."

20 And likewise, the cup after they had eaten, saying, "This cup that is poured out for you is the new covenant in my blood.

Jesus also implemented the ritual of foot washing. This was practised in the earlier church. Many churches today have ceased this practice. Many churches today want to be above and beyond the world, as you have seen. Humility is practised by only a few people, both inside and outside the church. In truth, it's often practised by the poor in spirit. Remember that the so-called "Christian" can't match the world.

John 13:1-17

King James Version

13 Now before the feast of the Passover, when Jesus knew that his hour was come that he should depart out of this world unto the Father, having loved his own which were in the world, he loved them unto the end.

2 And supper being ended, the devil having now put into the heart of Judas Iscariot, Simon's son, to betray him;

3 Jesus, knowing that the Father had given all things into his hands, and that he had come from God, and went to God;

4 He riseth from supper, and laid aside his garments; and took a towel, and girded himself.

5 After that, he poureth water into a bason, and began to wash the disciples' feet, and to wipe them with the towel wherewith he was girded.

6 Then cometh he to Simon Peter: and Peter saith unto him, Lord, dost thou wash my feet?

7 Jesus answered and said unto him, What I do thou knowest not now; but thou shalt know hereafter.

8 Peter saith unto him, Thou shalt never wash my feet. Jesus answered him, If I wash thee not, thou hast no part with me.

9 Simon Peter saith unto him, Lord, not my feet only, but also my hands and my head.

10 Jesus saith to him, He that is washed needeth not save to wash his feet, but is clean every whit: and ye are clean, but not all.

11 For he knew who should betray him; therefore said he, Ye are not all clean.

12 So after he had washed their feet, and had taken his garments, and was set down again, he said unto them, Know ye what I have done to you?

13 Ye call me Master and Lord: and ye say well; for so I am.

14 If I then, your Lord and Master, have washed your feet; ye also ought to wash one another's feet.

15 For I have given you an example, that ye should do as I have done to you.

16 Verily, verily, I say unto you, The servant is not greater than his lord; neither he that is sent greater than he that sent him.

17 If ye know these things, happy are ye if ye do them.

Garden of Gethsemane

Apart from the Garden of Eden, the second most popular garden in the Bible is Gethsemane. This garden is associated with betrayal and temptation. It was in this garden that Judas Iscariot, the son of Simon, kissed Jesus as a sign to the Romans that he was the Messiah or the one to be arrested—this signalled betrayal, although it had been pre-planned by Judas and the high priests of the Temple. Without Judas, Jesus wouldn't have been crucified. Jesus had already told his disciples that he chose twelve, and one of them is a devil (see John 6:70). It was common in Jesus' time for the Rabbi to kiss his student, not for the student to kiss the Rabbi. That's why Jesus said to Judas, "You betray the Son of Man with a kiss."

This is also the garden where Jesus was on two occasions. Should he be crucified, or should he walk away? It is said that Jesus' sweat became like blood in this garden because of the excellent task ahead. After all, Jesus' primary purpose was to atone for sins, but it wasn't as easy in the final hour. A lot of important decisions had to be made and made fast.

Jesus went along with his disciples to this garden to fast and pray. Jesus prayed and fasted while his disciples couldn't keep up. The others, apart from

Judas, were clueless about what was going to happen a few hours later. Jesus knew beforehand. Jesus told his disciples before, but it seemed they'd forgotten. Betrayal and crucifixion didn't take him by surprise. Jesus encouraged the disciples to fast and pray for even an hour. They said 'yes', but minutes later, they were fast asleep. Their bodies needed sleep. They chose to obey their flesh rather than the Spirit, which bid them pray and fast for the hour draweth nigh.

Jesus asked the Father what His will was. Should he die or should he call for ten thousand angels to defend him? After all, why should he die for these rogue people? Why did he leave heaven's glory? Was this a mistake? After all, it wasn't too late to admit He was wrong. This was the human side that thought about all these things. This is the carnal mind. From the scripture, we know the carnal mind is enmity against God (see Romans 8:7). This means that carnality cannot please God. Morality, civility, traditions of men, legality, human philosophy, and vain reasoning cannot please God. These things are useless before the Kings of Kings and Lords of Lords.

Jesus prayed for the cup of suffering and humiliation to be passed from him. He prayed to have this bitter cup removed from before his face. Jesus also showed us an example. Jesus didn't pray for his own will, but for the will of God to prevail in his life. Jesus' prayers aligned with Scripture and context (see Romans 8:26). These prayers weren't filled with carnality or human desires. What's God's will for my life? God doesn't necessarily need to reveal His will to us for us to pray for His will. God doesn't reveal everything to us. God doesn't even tell the apostles and prophets everything (see 1 Corinthians 13:9). God reveals only in part to us. In part, it simply means that everything is not known to us. For example, you were born again last week, but God doesn't tell you what you will be in 3, 6, 9, or even 12 months from now. If God doesn't reveal it, you can't know it. However, if we follow and abide in God's word, then His will is fulfilled in us. Jesus told his disciples that if they abide in him, they will bear much fruit. Not just plenty of fruit, but good fruit (see John 15:7). Sometimes we are producing fruit, but it's not good fruit. Jesus also highlighted that a good tree produces good fruit. The bad tree produces evil or bad fruit (Matthew 7:17-20). We should be careful of the fruit we are bearing in church, school, at home, at work, on the streets, and most importantly, before the Lord Jesus himself. We must remember that God is a Spirit. God is life. And God is the one who will judge both living and dead (see 2 Timothy 4:1; Revelation 20:12).

Jesus Christ had overcome all these things (see John 16:33). The Garden of Gethsemane made him more fervent in prayer. The Father didn't spare him from crucifixion because that was the perfect will of God (see Romans 8:32-35). Jesus hadn't come this far to give up now.

Matthew 26:36-46 English Standard Version (ESV)

Jesus Prays in Gethsemane

36 Then Jesus went with them to a place called Gethsemane, and he said to his disciples, "Sit here, while I go over there and pray."

37 And taking with him Peter and the two sons of Zebedee, he began to be sorrowful and troubled.

38 Then he said to them, "My soul is very sorrowful, even to death; remain here, and watch with me."

39 And going a little farther he fell on his face and prayed, saying, "My Father, if it be possible, let this cup pass from me; nevertheless, not as I will, but as you will."

40 And he came to the disciples and found them sleeping. And he said to Peter, "So, could you not watch with me one hour?

41 Watch and pray that you may not enter into temptation. The spirit indeed is willing, but the flesh is weak."

42 Again, for the second time, he went away and prayed, "My Father, if this cannot pass unless I drink it, your will be done."

43 And again he came and found them sleeping, for their eyes were heavy.

44 So, leaving them again, he went away and prayed for the third time, repeating the exact words.

45 Then he came to the disciples and said to them, "Sleep and take your rest later on. See, the hour is at hand, and the Son of Man is betrayed into the hands of sinners.

46 Rise, let us be going; see, my betrayer, is at hand."

The Crucifixion

Crucifixion is a method of punishment or capital punishment in which the victim is tied or nailed to a large wooden beam and left to hang, perhaps for several days, until eventual death from exhaustion and asphyxiation. It has been used as a punishment in parts of the world as recently as the twentieth century.

The crucifixion of Jesus is central to Christianity, and the cross (sometimes depicting Jesus nailed to it) is the central religious symbol for many Christian churches.

Ancient Greek has two verbs for crucify: anastauro (ἀνασταυρόω), from stauros (which in today's Greek only means "cross" but which in antiquity was used of any wooden pole, pointed or blunt, bare or with attachments) and apotumpanizo (ἀποτυμπανίζω) "crucify on a plank", together with anaskolopizo (ἀνασκολοπίζω "impale").

In earlier pre-Roman Greek texts, anastauro usually means "impale".

New Testament Greek uses four verbs, three of which are based on stauros (σταυρός), usually translated "cross". The most common term is stauroo (σταυρόω), "to crucify", occurring 46 times; sustauroo (συσταυρόω), "to crucify with" or "alongside" appears five times, while anastauroo (ἀνασταυρόω), "to crucify again" appears only once at the Epistle to the Hebrews 6:6. Prospegnumi (προσπήγνυμι), "to fix or fasten to, impale, crucify" appears only once at the Acts of the Apostles 2:23.

The English term cross derives from the Latin word "crux", which classically referred to a tree or any construction of wood used to hang criminals as a form of execution. The term later came to refer specifically to a cross.

The English term crucifix derives from the Latin crucifixus or cruci fixus, past participle passive of crucifigere or cruci figere, meaning "to crucify" or "to fasten to a cross".

Crucifixion was most often performed to dissuade its witnesses from perpetrating similar (usually particularly heinous) crimes. Victims were sometimes left on display after death as a warning to any other potential criminals. Crucifixion was typically intended to provide a death that was particularly slow, painful (hence the term excruciating, literally "out of crucifying"), gruesome, humiliating, and public, using whatever means were most expedient for that goal. Crucifixion methods varied considerably with location and time.

The Greek and Latin words corresponding to "crucifixion" applied to many different forms of painful execution, including being impaled on a stake, or affixed to a tree, upright pole (a crux simplex), or (most famous now) to a combination of an upright (in Latin, stipes) and a crossbeam (in Latin, patibulum). Seneca the Younger wrote: "I see crosses there, not just of one kind but made in many different ways: some have their victims with head down to the ground; some impale their private parts; others stretch out their arms on the gibbet".

In some cases, the condemned was forced to carry the crossbeam to the place of execution. A whole cross would weigh well over 135 kg (300 lb), but the crossbeam would not be as burdensome, weighing around 45 kg (100 lb). The Roman historian Tacitus records that the city of Rome had a specific place for carrying out executions, situated outside the Esquiline Gate, and had a specific area reserved for the execution of enslaved people by crucifixion. Upright posts would presumably be fixed permanently in that place, and the crossbeam, with the condemned person perhaps already nailed to it, would then be attached to the post.

The person executed may have been attached to the cross by rope. However, nails and other sharp materials are mentioned in a passage by the Judean historian Josephus, where he states that at the Siege of Jerusalem (AD70), "the soldiers out of rage and hatred, nailed those they caught, one after one way, and another after another, to the crosses, by way of jest". Objects used in the crucifixion of criminals, such as nails, were sought as amulets with perceived medicinal qualities.

While a crucifixion was an execution, it was also a humiliation, by making the condemned as vulnerable as possible. Although artists have traditionally depicted the figure on a cross with a loincloth or a covering of the genitals, the person being crucified was usually stripped naked. Writings by Seneca the Younger state that some victims suffered a stick forced upwards through their groin. Despite its frequent use by the Romans, the horrors of crucifixion did not escape criticism by some eminent Roman orators. Cicero, for example, described crucifixion as "a most cruel and disgusting punishment" and suggested that "the very mention of the cross should be far removed not only from a Roman citizen's body, but from his mind, his eyes, and his ears". Elsewhere, he says, "It is a crime to bind a Roman citizen; to scourge him is a wickedness; to put him to death is almost parricide. What shall I say of crucifying him? So guilty an action cannot by any possibility be adequately expressed by any name bad enough for it."

Frequently, the legs of the person executed were broken or shattered with an iron club, an act called crurifragium, which was also often applied without crucifixion to slaves. This act hastened the death of the person but was also meant to deter those who observed the crucifixion from committing offences.

The Scripture mentions that Jesus Christ was crucified by the Romans.

The introduction of crucifixion highlights what kind of punishment it was. It was capital punishment. This was the method of punishment that the Romans used to execute Jesus. He was nailed to a cross, but his bones were not broken based on prophecy (see Psalm 34:20 and Psalm 22:16). The crucifixion of Christ is not debatable because it's written in scripture. In truth and fairness, we can't go against what is written. We can't say Jesus wasn't crucified because that makes no sense to us. Or Jesus was shipped off to India, while another man who looked like him was on the cross. All these arguments are like building a house on the sand. Building your house on the sand will end in destruction. However, if you build your house on the rock, which is truth, you will stand the storms of life and the storms of false doctrines (see Luke 6:48). All four gospels tell the story of the crucifixion. We are not here trying to prove the crucifixion; we are highlighting the accounts. We don't need to prove anything to anyone. In truth, what we should do is to believe in the truth even more. Christ didn't call us to join senseless debating groups to prove whether he was crucified or not, or resurrected or not. Many individuals spend their lives in this manner of debate. If you go on the many so-called Christian pages on Social Media, oftentimes you will see and hear endless debates on simple stuff. These are the people who think they are preaching and teaching the gospel of Jesus Christ, but in truth, they are working for Satan and his kingdom. The apostle Paul warned us that debates should never be a part of the church (see Titus 3:9; Romans 14:1; Colossians 2:1 - 2:23).

Concerning the case for Christ, it's solely an act of faith along with works, as James chapter 2 highlights. Faith, in truth, without works is dead (see James 2:26). We can't prove that Christ was crucified today easily, even if we find an empty tomb. We can't prove it. The question remains: why do we then preach and teach it? The truth is that the Bible was written by eyewitnesses to the events it records. These are firsthand accounts. These eyewitnesses didn't have video cameras, Social Media accounts, or the Internet. They saw it with their physical eyes. They had nothing to gain by saying Jesus was crucified if he indeed wasn't. They had nothing to gain by saying he was resurrected if he wasn't resurrected. It's not like they were given money to sell fake news as seen today. Remember that Jesus Christ wasn't a Christian. Jesus didn't form Christianity. Jesus didn't say become Christians. He didn't say to form different religions, denominations, creeds, and churches. These are the truths people don't like to hear. Christianity was formed later by the HOLY ROMAN EMPIRE. There is a history of Christianity, just as there is of all things. Even God has a certain history. What Jesus Christ came to do was to fulfil the Law and Prophets. The Law is known as Torat Moshe or the Law of Moses. It's also called the Torah. The Prophets are known as Nevi'im. This is what Christ came and fulfilled. Everything that the Torah and prophets spoke about him.

Some Say He Has Not Risen

Religion is a system of beliefs in a god or goddess. To become born again is a different thing. To become born again means to put on Christ, walk in Christ, believe in Christ and have the power in Christ. To follow religion does not equate to following or obeying Jesus Christ. Be mindful that one's religion can be vain. One can be following traditions and creeds, but not Christ Jesus the Lord.

The reason why I highlighted *religion* versus being *born again* is that the reader should become aware that they aren't the same thing, and that if you follow religion, then you'll not make it anywhere in the true spiritual sense. I want to highlight one of the world's major religions: Islam. Now, in Islam, they believe in Jesus Christ as the Messiah, who was to come as prophesied by the prophets. They believe Jesus was a holy prophet of God or of "Allah." They believe Mary was his mother and that he performed many miracles. They believe that Jesus will return in the end to judge and redeem the world. All these things are true according to the biblical scriptures and what is prophesied. However, Islam doesn't believe in the resurrection of Jesus Christ. First, Islam doesn't support the view that Jesus was crucified, nor did he die for our sins and was raised as written in the scriptures. Islam believes that Jesus Christ went away to India, and that the person who the people saw on the cross wasn't Jesus Christ but another person. In other words, "Allah" sent delusion on the people so that it only appeared that they had killed Jesus Christ when, in fact, he disappeared into India.

This theory in Islam is treated as "gospel." But why would Islam not believe in the crucifixion and resurrection of Jesus Christ? After all, they believe all this great stuff about "Prophet Jesus." They believe some of the truth, but not the entire truth. As we get deeper into this book, you'll see, from a biblical perspective, that without the power and belief in the resurrection of Christ Jesus, you're rendered powerless. Whereas we can believe in all the good things that Jesus did and what he'll do, it is futile not to believe in his resurrection.

Islam doesn't believe in the resurrection power, and they don't have it. They don't believe Jesus Christ died and rose from the dead for our sins. In truth, I know someone else who hates the resurrection, but knows it's true and accurate, and that's Satan, who is the enemy of Man. Satan has blinded the eyes of people from the knowledge of the truth in Christ because he is the god of this world and the deceiver. Imagine if all those millions of Muslims had believed Jesus Christ died and rose from the dead, and he died for their sins, and the sins of the world, then Satan's kingdom would be shattered further in pieces. The truth is, many millions will not believe.

But the truth is that they don't believe, thus they are rendered spiritually powerless. By believing and accepting the resurrection, light will become a part of your life. All the lies you're told will vanish and become obsolete. No one who believes in the resurrection is weak or double-minded. They believe Jesus is Lord, not just a mere prophet. They believe Jesus is the Son of God, and by believing in him, they'll have an abundant life. They no longer walk in darkness; they now have the light of life (see John 8:12).

The fundamental thing here to remember is that Satan hates the resurrection power, which is in another category from his. Satan is powerless over all the children of the resurrection. When God's children die, they aren't dead but asleep. Satan can't capture their souls in hell as he does with those who have died in sin.

The example of Islam used here is one of the many religions which denounce the crucifixion and resurrection of Jesus Christ. Outside of Christianity, no other sector of society believes Jesus was raised from the dead. This issue isn't new to the scriptures. The apostle Paul gives us a good illustration in 1 Corinthians 15, where he discusses the credibility of the resurrection of Jesus Christ. There were many in his day who walked around spreading lies known as heresies. They were saying Jesus wasn't resurrected from the dead. They said that, although they were baptised, their hope was vain. The apostle Paul had to rebuke these heresies and remind the converts that if Jesus hadn't been raised from the dead, their faith would've been vain or hopeless. Some converts were even baptising for the dead, which the apostle rebuked as well. Many strange doctrines and concepts had crept into the Corinthian church, which the apostle had to rebuke and cast out. No doubt Satan was the one who had blinded the eyes of the new converts so that they felt like Christ wasn't raised, and their faith was vain. However, God used the apostle to revive their belief in the resurrection.

Touching the crucifixion of Jesus Christ, Muslims believe he wasn't crucified, but he was sent off to India, and those people who saw "Jesus" on the cross at Calvary didn't see him but saw someone who looked like him. In other words, there was a substitution. Why would God allow this? Muslims conclude Jesus was innocent of any crimes. However, this doesn't make any sense. In truth, this is heresy. There are also various books stating he was in India, and I can proudly say none of them were inspired by the Holy Ghost. This is a false doctrine. Here are several reasons why this is false and Jesus wasn't in India:

1. God shifted Jesus off to India. **In truth, why would Jesus Christ go to India when his mission was to go to the lost sheep of Israel? Also, the disciples saw Jesus as he was taken up into heaven in a cloud. Jesus would have been the world's biggest liar if**

he said he was going to heaven but ran off to India, deceiving the disciples. The entire New Testament would have to be rewritten because of the heresy. (See John 10:11, 15, 17-18, *Luke 23:33, Matthew 27:54, John 19:30, and 1 Peter 3:18.*

2. Jesus Christ wasn't on the cross for us, but another man who resembled him, and the crowds didn't know. **God allowed a sinner to be a substitute for us to die for our sins. If God allowed this, then no one's sins are forgiven. Everyone who has passed already would still be in their sins. What this would mean is deception. God tells us we are forgiven, but no one's sin is forgiven** (see Romans 5:6-8, Galatians 1:3-5, 1 John 4:10, and 1 Corinthians 15:3).

3. **God has no begotten Son.** This belief is also heresy. The Bible tells us that the Son of Man came to seek and to save that which was lost (see John 3: 16).

The Power Within

When we say power, we talk about extraordinary abilities. Many of us, as children growing up, would be familiar with heroes such as Superman, Green Lantern, Captain America, and the list goes on and on. These heroes are figments of our imagination. They were made up to keep us happy. Everyone wanted to be probably like Batman, the Flash, and the man of steel himself- Superman. They certainly had extraordinary abilities. Superman, for example, can melt steel with rays from his eyes, and he can lift heavy stuff. Even today, many TV shows and books are highlighted based on these fictitious heroes. You probably also had real heroes, such as your father, brother, or granddad, or even heroines.

As children of God or children of the resurrection of Jesus Christ, we, too, have powers within. First, we need to understand that our power comes from Christ Jesus the Lord. The power we have isn't to shoot physical fire from our eyes or even to lift heavy stuff, but it is to speak whatever we want into being. "WHATEVER" means anything we imagine. "WHATEVER" doesn't have any limit. Jesus said to his disciples, "Whatever you ask in my name I'll do it." This power lies in the name of Jesus Christ. At the name of Jesus Christ, every knee shall bow. Everything tongue confess that He is Lord and

God (see Philippians 2:10). Jesus also said, "Behold, I give you power over all serpents and dragons. And all the power over the enemy." (See Luke 10:19). Imagine for a moment if Jesus Christ hadn't given us power. Technically, we'd be subdued by the enemy and the demonic world every time we preach, testify, and teach about Jesus. Jesus sent out his disciples two by two, giving them power over the enemy and the authority to do whatever they wanted. He said to heal the sick, raise the dead, set free those who are bound, and more. When the disciples returned, they were overjoyed by the power and stuff they could do by just saying the word and the name of Jesus Christ. This was Christ's power working in them.

There are two types of powers in this world: those of Satan and the demonic kingdom, and those of God and Christ. Humans are only given these powers to use. The kingdom of darkness is reached by the works of the flesh mentioned in Galatians 5. The main job of the flesh that evokes satanic power is witchcraft. Wherever and whenever witchcraft is practised, it evokes demonic enmities of various kinds and creeds. Practising these rituals can lead to demonic possession and all other types of attacks. The demonic world is ruled by unforgiveness. There's no pardon or second chance if you fail the first time. Yet these powers may look powerful to those who aren't of the resurrection power. The people of the world may be in "awe." Do you recall the story of Simon the sorcerer in Acts chapter 8?

Simon was a practising sorcerer who bewitched the people of Samaria. The people thought he was a great man until Philip the Evangelist, a deacon, went and preached everything concerning Jesus Christ and the kingdom of God. When the people heard Philip's preaching, they were baptised, both men and women. Not only were these people baptised, but the sorcerer too was converted and baptised in the name of the Lord Jesus after hearing the evangelist's preaching about Christ's kingdom. Simon realised that the power of Christ was far superior to the power of darkness. He realised this to the very extent that when the apostle Peter and John came to Samaria to lay their hands on those who should receive the Holy Ghost, he said to Peter, "Sell me this power that whosoever I lay my hands on they'll receive the Holy Ghost."

The Acts of the Apostles, chapter 10, tells us how God anointed Jesus of Nazareth with the power of the Holy Ghost and how he went about doing good (see Acts 10:38). Notice that Jesus didn't go about doing evil or showing favouritism to people. Everywhere he went, he did well. Jesus didn't say no to those who came to him. The Pharisees and Sadducees hated Jesus because he healed people on the Sabbath.

The Resurrection

The resurrection of Jesus Christ represents power. There are various types of resurrection highlighted in the Scripture. I'm not talking only about the instances of the resurrection but the forms of them. The Bible describes the resurrection from dead works. This resurrection is when your life is entirely free from sin. You're dead to sin and alive to righteousness in Jesus. The Bible also speaks of the First Resurrection, as described in Revelation 20. This resurrection is that of all born-again believers who have ever lived on earth. These believers who are dead will be raised to life by the power of the Spirit which is in them. At the time of this writing, this resurrection hasn't yet taken place.

The other resurrection is the Second Resurrection, also described in Revelation 20. This resurrection occurs after the millennial reign of Jesus Christ on earth, when all nations are subjected to him. This resurrection is for the dead who died as sinners. They died without the hope of the First Resurrection. They died outside of Christ and are hopeless. They died without the active Spirit of Jesus Christ. They are raised in corruption as described in 1 Corinthians 15. If their hearts were sinless and exemplary, they would've been raised with Christ, but no, they died corrupted by sin and transgression.

These are the murderers, fornicators, adulterers, disobedient to parents, thieves, drunkards, and the list goes on and on. These are raised bodily to life, nonetheless to face the judgment of Almighty God in the Great White Throne Judgment.

The purpose of the resurrection

The purpose of the resurrection is to give us another chance at life. Not just life but eternal life. When God created this world, He created human beings. He gave humans a command that they shouldn't eat from the tree of the knowledge of good and evil. A few moments later, Adam and Eve happily ate from the forbidden fruit. God punished them, and because of disobedience to His word, sin entered this world. Death also came into the world. Remember that previously, Satan and a third of the angels sinned against God and were kicked out of heaven. Sin was in heaven, but it didn't impact the earth. Sin came on earth by someone from the world, not heaven. Satan tricked Eve into picking and eating the fruit. Sin and death go hand in hand. The truth is the wages of sin is death. The gift of God is eternal life. God didn't want Adam and Eve to live forever in a sinful state, so He sent cherubim of fire to guard the tree of life. The truth is, the last evil would be greater than the first if people were to live forever in sin. God gives His beloved sleep (Psalm 127). Wherever *sleep* is mentioned in the Holy Bible as a non-figurative word, it refers to resting from torment. It is used to identify the children of God who aren't described as *dead* but *resting from their labour* (Revelation 14:13). The unsaved dead aren't described as *asleep*; they are described as *dead*.

A Glorious Body

Those who die in Jesus will receive a glorious body that is just like the Lord's resurrected body. And this is only possible because Jesus Christ came into the world and died for our sins and was raised on the third day as a man unspotted from the world. We can't enter the kingdom of heaven without knowing and accepting Jesus as Lord of our lives. Adam and Eve couldn't have lived forever on this earth, nor could they have entered heaven. Remember, the name Jesus wasn't revealed to them. We aren't even sure that they knew God's name. They didn't even know much about God. Likely, they didn't know much about God or anything at all about him. We can assume this based on what the serpent said to Eve. The serpent could have easily tricked the woman into doubting God's words. He didn't even have to move to plan B because plan A was enough. What Satan did was make the woman doubt God's word. For example, if you know someone well, you wouldn't doubt them. Would you doubt your wife or husband if they are faithful to you for many years? No, I think you wouldn't. In truth, what the serpent did was ask: 'What do you know about God?' 'See, He told you not to eat this fruit, but who knows what He's hiding from you. This fruit will make you wise just like gods. Not wise like 'God' but 'gods.' The serpent told a half-truth and a half-lie. He told the truth about becoming just like 'gods', but the other part he deliberately left out was the consequences of having this knowledge. Sin and death came with it. You must understand that Satan has corrupted wisdom.

That He May Present Us Faultless Before the Father

Christ lived an exemplary life for us to follow. But does this mean that before the time of Christ, people lived contrary to righteousness? Well, the truth is that before Christ, many people lived contrary to the law of righteousness. This is the reason why Christ came so that all who lived righteously before Him could be set free by the resurrection in Him. Without Christ's death, burial, and resurrection, there would be no resurrection. All the prophets of God who lived, preached and prophesied their works would be for nought if there were no resurrection.

Judaism on the Resurrection of Jesus Christ

Today, there is only a small number of Jews across the world who believe and accept that Jesus Christ is Lord and God. Some of these Jews are from the U.S.A, the Middle East, Africa, the Caribbean, and Latin America. The time of Jesus Christ was filled with Jews and descendants of Israel. Many who believed in Jesus Christ were Jewish. Jesus Christ called no one "Christian." "Christian" was never used during Jesus' time on earth. Jesus preached and taught in the Synagogue on the Sabbath day. Jesus Christ did good on the Sabbath day. Jesus healed people on the Sabbath day.

It was after Jesus ascended into heaven, which, in truth, was many years later, that people used the word "Christian" to mean simply a follower of Christ. This was first used in the city of Antioch in ancient Turkey (see Acts 11:26). Tradition stated this was the location of the first Gentile church. Gentile means "non-Jew," or one born outside of the descendants of Israel or the commonwealth of Israel. Today, you also have the term "secular Jew", which is used for those Jews who aren't religious.

Back to our original theme. In Jesus' day, the Pharisees and Sadducees didn't believe in him. The

Pharisees were a group of about 70 men who gave religious instruction to the people of Israel. They seldom practised what they preached. They were not prophets, but rather more like priests. Priests and prophets in the Bible were often at odds with one another. Only a few of the priests worshipped and obeyed God. Most of them didn't. Prophets, however, did everything God told them to do. These were the prophets of the Most High God.

The Sadducees didn't believe in the resurrection of the dead. They, too, were Jews. They didn't believe in Jesus Christ either. Jesus often was in debates with both these groups who observed his teachings, conduct, and manner.

It wasn't the Jews who had Jesus crucified. It was God's will that made it happen. Without God's consent, we can't do anything. From a historical point of view, it may seem that the Jews, Herod, and the Romans put him on the cross, but spiritually God did. This, in truth, is of the greatest significance. He became sin for us who knew NO SIN. He became the Lamb of God who took away the sin of the world. Jesus made mention that no one takes his life from him, but he gives it up freely (John 10:18).

Modern Judaism

Today, in the year 2019, many Jews don't believe in Jesus Christ as the Messiah. Just as in the ancient days, when the Pharisees and Sadducees mentioned that the Messiah wouldn't and didn't come from a place called Nazareth. Many Jews today are still waiting for their Messiah. The Messiah is supposed to bring them out of bondage and restore all good things. In Israel today, many have this hope. They are not all wrong. The Messiah will bring those things to pass, but he must also suffer those things which are prophesied in Scripture. No one who truly studies the Bible would deny the deity of Jesus Christ. The prophets of the Old Testament prophesied that the nation of Israel would see Jesus Christ but believe in someone else. They know, deep down, that he is Lord and God, but chooses to do and worship otherwise. Isaiah prophesied of them in that manner.

Today, there are over 300 prophecies about Jesus Christ, and some are yet to be fulfilled. Christ's Millennial reign is yet to be fulfilled. This is the 1,000 years of Christ when he will rule the nations in peace, love, and righteousness. Everyone will worship God and learn about Him. There are a few others that are still not fulfilled, and these probably are roughly 10 per cent. 90% of the Bible is already fulfilled.

Why won't the Jews of today believe?

To believe isn't as easy as it sounds. Belief kills, and it cures, as the saying goes. The main reason why the Jews of today don't believe in Jesus is that they are still stuck in the traditions of their forefathers. Once human tradition is present on earth, people will hardly believe in God. Traditions are mostly human-based. For example, a popular Jewish tradition is to worship and rest on the Sabbath. For Christians, it would be to worship on a Sunday. The non-traditionalist will worship God on any day. He doesn't have any set days. Tradition can and has encompassed many things. This is what Jesus Christ said about human tradition. For example, in which of the Bible did God tell people to worship Him on the Sabbath day? You can't find one passage, yet some Christians and Jews worship God on that day.

Mark 7:7-13 King James Version (KJV)

[7] Howbeit in vain do they worship me, teaching for doctrines the commandments of men.

[8] For laying aside the commandment of God, ye hold the tradition of men, as the washing of pots and cups: and many other such like things ye do.

[9] And he said unto them, Full well ye reject the commandment of God, that ye may keep your own tradition.

[10] For Moses said, Honour thy father and thy mother; and, Whoso curseth father or mother, let him die the death:

[11] But ye say, If a man shall say to his father or mother, It is Corban, that is to say, a gift, by

whatsoever thou mightest be profited by me; he shall be free.

¹² And ye suffer him no more to do ought for his father or his mother;

¹³ Making the word of God of no effect through your tradition, which ye have delivered: and many such like things do ye.

Tradition as a topic can be a book by itself. Jesus Christ, in the above chapter, told the Pharisees that their humanistic traditions prevented them from comprehending the things of God. It hindered their spiritual bucket of faith from being filled. It hindered them from seeing that eating with unwashed hands wasn't sinful, although they thought it was. Jesus healed people on the Sabbath, and tradition stated that what he did was wrong. Jesus asked them if it was better to do evil on the Sabbath or to do good. They didn't know because their tradition said otherwise. In their tradition, doing good on the Sabbath day was considered absolute evil.

Some scriptures where Jesus healed on the Sabbath day.

Luke 13:14

And the ruler of the synagogue answered with indignation, because that Jesus had healed on the sabbath day, and said unto the people, There are six days in which men ought to work: in them therefore come and be healed, and not on the sabbath day.

Mark 2:24

And the Pharisees said unto him, Behold, why do they on the sabbath day that which is not   lawful?

Mark 3:2

And they watched him, whether he would heal him on the sabbath day; that they might accuse him.

John 5:9

And immediately the man was made whole, and took up his bed, and walked: and on the same day was the sabbath.

Conclusion

Tradition encompasses everything. For example, dressing, talking, marriage, work fields, singing, and everything we can think of. Tradition is the way of life for many people and their families. The Pharisees held to their traditions, and it blinded their eyes. If the Jews of today have to this kind of tradition, they'll not believe or accept the fact that Jesus Christ is Lord, God, and the promised Messiah.

The Law of God doesn't go by any human tradition, mindset, or ambition. If one were to think of God's tradition, it would have to be holiness and righteousness. But because humans, in general, tend to do religious traditions that bring no real spiritual change, much is hindered. Today, much of the church's downfall stems from its adherence to human tradition each Sunday or Saturday when it gathers to worship. These, in truth, are the multiplexed denominations or religions as they are called in some countries. They say they worship one God, but there are millions of denominations all professing stuff that they assume God told them to do.

The Holy Spirit was given to those who believe so that they wouldn't be traditionalized in the ways of man or people. The Holy Spirit is like the wind that blows. You feel the wind, but you can't tell where it comes from. This minute, the wind is here, and the next, it's gone. Have you heard the statement: "gone like the wind?" Probably, just probably, you have heard it being said before. This is what Jesus Christ explained to Nicodemus, the Jewish master teacher of Israel. The good analogy here is that Nicodemus was a Jewish master teacher, but he couldn't understand the things of the Spirit. The things of the Spirit seemed like nonsense to him. That's the case when you're spiritually blind, maimed, and dumb. The Spirit is a mystery that can't be predicted. You can't expect that the Holy Spirit will send rain tomorrow on the dry, thirsty land unless it is made known by the Spirit itself. It simply doesn't work in the order of men or humanistic thinking.

It's the same thing in this present generation. You may have a nation of people, but the truth is that only a remnant will be saved from death, sin, and destruction. There are quite a few million Jews today scattered around the world. The majority are in Israel. Out of those millions of Jewish people in Israel, only 12,000 will be sealed with the mark of God from each tribe. The mark of God is the Holy Spirit. This is what seals the people of God from the wrath of the Lamb.

Ephesians 1:13 King James Version (KJV)

13 In whom ye also trusted, after that, ye heard the word of truth, the gospel of your salvation: in whom also after that ye believed, ye were sealed with that holy Spirit of promise,

2 Timothy 2:19-21 King James Version (KJV)

19 Nevertheless, the foundation of God standeth sure, having this seal, The Lord knoweth them that are his. And let everyone that nameth the name of Christ depart from iniquity.

20 But in a great house there are not only vessels of gold and of silver, but also of wood and of earth; and some to honour, and some to dishonour.

21 If a man, therefore, purge himself from these, he shall be a vessel unto honour, sanctified, and meet for the master's use, and prepared unto every good work.

Revelation 7-11 English Standard Version (ESV)

The 144,000 of Israel Sealed

7 After this I saw four angels standing at the four corners of the earth, holding back the four winds of the earth, that no wind might blow on earth or sea or against any tree.

[2] Then I saw another angel ascending from the rising of the sun, with the seal of the living God, and he called with a loud voice to the four angels who had been given power to harm earth and sea,

³ saying, "Do not harm the earth or the sea or the trees, until we have sealed the servants of our God on their foreheads."

⁴ And I heard the number of the sealed, 144,000, sealed from every tribe of the sons of Israel:

⁵ 12,000 from the tribe of Judah were sealed,
12,000 from the tribe of Reuben,
12,000 from the tribe of Gad,
⁶ 12,000 from the tribe of Asher,
12,000 from the tribe of Naphtali,
12,000 from the tribe of Manasseh,
⁷ 12,000 from the tribe of Simeon,
12,000 from the tribe of Levi,
12,000 from the tribe of Issachar,
⁸ 12,000 from the tribe of Zebulun,
12,000 from the tribe of Joseph,
12,000 from the tribe of Benjamin were sealed.

The truth is God loves us all. However, there will come a time when we must choose whether we will love Him as well. God knows us by His Spirit. He has sealed us with His Holy Spirit so that we can reign with Him in glory.

If the Jews of today believe in this Gospel, they too can be saved and be set free. No one is set free and chooses to remain the same. It begins with hearing the word of faith and believing in repentance. It's because of a lack of faith that the anti-Christ will come on the earth and deceive many. Some of these people, based on their actions, want to be deceived.

The truth is, the Lord knows those whom He has prepared. He knows those who are ready. He knows those who are getting ready. He knows those who are fast asleep. He knows those who are drunk. He knows those who preach the gospel insincerely. He knows those who are preaching the gospel for fame and greed. He knows those who are preaching another gospel. He knows all things. He knows what we'll do tomorrow, the next second from now, the next day, the next five years, etc. Nothing takes the Almighty by surprise. The word here is "omniscient", meaning all-knowing or knowing everything in the past, present, and future. If God didn't know all things, he wouldn't have revealed to his servant the things that must come shortly.

Revelation 1:18-20 King James Version (KJV)

[18] I am he that liveth, and was dead; and, behold, I am alive for evermore, Amen; and have the keys of hell and of death.

[19] Write the things which thou hast seen, and the things which are, and the things which shall be hereafter;

[20] The mystery of the seven stars which thou sawest in my right hand, and the seven golden candlesticks. The seven stars are the angels of the seven churches, and the seven candlesticks which thou sawest are the seven churches.

Contrary to what you may have heard or believed, the word of God bears witness to the truth. Are you sure you're not practising religion over righteousness? Lies over truth. Choosing Satan's laws over Jesus' grace? We need to examine ourselves and our beliefs. Sometimes we must unlearn certain things. Even history today in the 21st Century has become confusing. For example, history is supposed to be a record of factual events relating to a particular people and culture. But many things students have learned in history lessons, from primary to university level, have proven to be false. In truth, it couldn't have been realistic. They must unlearn most of that stuff. Some professors will tell you that it was the history of the time, but they know the truth. They know that history should be factual. The truth is that true history can't be changed. For example, you can't say that Spanish wasn't spoken first in Spain. You wouldn't know that Jamaica, Cuba, Grenada, and Haiti aren't a part of the Caribbean. A hundred years later, you can't say Jamaica didn't speak English, and Haiti didn't speak French. With modern technology, especially social media, we can weigh everything in the balance. The point I'm making here is that much of ancient history was speculation. They were not anything concrete. They were filled with assumptions. But you're told history is always proper, correct, and accurate.

For example, did you know historians, archaeologists, research scientists, and ordinary men, women, boys, and girls constantly debate who built the great pyramids of Egypt? They struggle with this because the majority believed it was the ancient Egyptians, and another set thought it was another group of people. Yet nearly all history books say pyramids were invented and built by the ancient Egyptians. The truth is that no writing or evidence in ancient Egyptian relics states that they invented or built the Great Pyramids. But with humans, we'll always speculate when we see the evidence, when we see only part of it, or even when we see no evidence.

Another lie you were probably told in history is that history was written as a sure way to trap or trick people. That's a blatant lie! They got this ideology and reasoning from the ancient Egyptians. It is said that the ancient Egyptians only recorded history that was favourable to them. For example, if they won a war, they would document it in their history, but if they lost a battle, they wouldn't. History was written to blind people's eyes. No, history was written based on assumptions about what people thought happened. This is why many history books have similar yet different accounts of the same story. The Bible is a historical book, but it's not 100 per cent historical in that sense. The Bible has a few historical accounts. Biblical history is only relevant to certain stuff. The Bible doesn't tell us what happened in South and Central America 2,000 or even 5,000 years ago, yet it tells us, in part, what was happening in the Middle East during that era. The Bible's purpose is to enlighten men from darkness to light. This is the main reason it was written. It wasn't written so you could get an A+ in history or an A in ancient religions. No, it was written so that you may believe that Jesus Christ is the Son of God, and by believing in His name, you may have eternal life (see John 20:31). The bestselling book in the world every year is the Holy Bible. The most popular book in the world is the Bible. The Bible is the only book to have been translated into every language of the world. The Bible is the only book in the world that is universal. Many countries swear on the Bible in court, though it's plain wrong, since Jesus said we should never swear by heaven, earth, or Jerusalem (see Matthew 5:34). We need to ask ourselves why we are swearing to God, since he knows all things.

John Bunyan wrote the second most popular book in the world, and it's "Pilgrim's Progress. It was written in the 1600s by a British pastor. It simply tells the story of the main character, Christian, and his journey to the Celestial City, another name for heaven. Christian was born in the City of Destruction, and he is tormented on various occasions by reading the Bible. By reading the Bible, he became aware that a great burden was on his back. Although his wife and children told him everything was alright, he knew it wasn't. He then met a man of good and noble character named Evangelist, who guided him on the path he should take. It's quite an interesting story. In our lives, we have often felt like Christians carrying a heavy burden. We must make tough decisions. For everything we can think of in life, there's a biblical scripture that can help. The Holy Bible is the only book that, after you have read it, you feel different. For example, you can just be finished reading superhero comic books, but still feel weak like a mouse. You read about how Superman is the Man of Steel, and how he can fly high in the sky. But when you're finished reading the comic, you don't feel any different. Do you feel any different? No! You still feel afraid, helpless, and torn. After reading the Holy Bible, you feel different because it isn't just words, but they are also streams of living water. Remember Jesus' words in John 4:14, "But whosoever drinketh of the water that I shall give him shall never thirst; but the water that I shall give him shall be in him a well of water springing up into everlasting life." There's life and power in God's word. Satan himself is afraid of the word of God. The word of God is the Sword of the Spirit. The sword cuts, divides, and conquers. God's word is also sure. Meaning even if you don't believe in God's words, they are still true and will still come to pass. After Jesus was tempted in the wilderness by the Tempter, Satan, he returned to Galilee in the power of the Spirit. Jesus overcame because the word of God was in his heart. One's crooked path can only be straightened by taking heed to God's word.

Luke 4:14

"And Jesus returned in the power of the Spirit into Galilee: and there went out a fame of him through all the region round about."

Psalms 119:9

"BETH. Wherewithal shall a young man cleanse his way? by taking heed thereto according to thy word."

True Believers Shall Live Again

Job 14:14

If a man die, shall he live again? all the days of my appointed time will I wait, till my change come.

Job 19:25

For I know that my redeemer liveth, and that he shall stand at the latter day upon the earth:

Matthew 25:23

His lord said unto him, Well done, good and faithful servant; thou hast been faithful over a few things, I will make thee ruler over many things: enter thou into the joy of thy lord.

When we think of resurrection in the scripture, we often think of the physical return of the dead to life. However, the scripture speaks of being resurrected on a spiritual level and being resurrected from dead works to live works. From sin to grace, etc. Despite the many scientific inventions and discoveries in various fields, scientists have yet to find a way for us to live forever. No plant, animal, or human can live forever on this current earth. One characteristic of all living things is growth. Once you're a living thing, you must grow. This is just one characteristic of living things. I could list more, but it's not necessary for this topic. We may take vitamins, dietary supplements, and do exercise, but these things don't prevent us from getting old or stop us from dying. In truth, it's a part of the journey. Sin brought death into this world. We can trace this from Genesis chapter 3. Adam and Eve ate from a tree they weren't supposed to have eaten from. It's important to know here that before they sinned, there was no death, accidents, old age, or anything sad and bad. There was evil, but it didn't affect them in any shape or form. Satan, in the form of a serpent, deceived Eve, and she encouraged Adam to eat from the tree himself. Both were together side by side. This was from the Tree of the Knowledge of Good and Evil. There was another tree called the Tree of Life. If they had eaten from that tree, they would have lived forever and ever in sin and transgressions. All the wicked people in Earth's past would still be around today. The Nephilim would still be around. Mighty men of renown would still be ruling this earth. For many of us who are sick in both body and mind, we'd still be in that condition forever. The world in such a form would be a lot more negative than it is today. God knew this, and he placed cherubim with flaming swords to guard the tree from anyone who would be tempted to touch the very bark or leaves. The Tree of Life was spiritual, though in a physical form. Anyone who felt it would be immortal. They would never die.

A lot of people don't understand what eternity means. The human mind, as it is, can't comprehend eternity. We can't see beyond the great beyond. Humans can only make plans and hope to stick to them. A man doesn't know when he'll die unless God makes it known. Satan himself doesn't know your future or when you'll die. Satan only acts on clues and thinks about them. Satan is like a detective.

We have hope of the resurrection today only because of Jesus Christ. Without Jesus Christ dying and rising from the dead, he would have become what is called the "first fruit of the resurrection." This is the hope of us who die also in Christ Jesus. As a born-again person, it shouldn't matter how, when, or where we die once we die in Jesus Christ. We don't need to study and know rocket science to believe in the resurrection of the dead. No, we must believe in Jesus.

The brethren in Corinth and Thessaloniki were ignorant of the resurrection of the dead. When we are babes in Christ, we're often ignorant and need a spiritual teacher. The Holy Spirit teaches us what we should know. God uses Spirit-filled pastors, teachers, apostles, prophets, evangelists, and the like also to show and teach us the way we should often go. God had to use the apostle Paul to reveal the truth to these brethren in Corinth, Rome, Thessaloniki, and the like. God used him because the brethren always mourned as those who had no hope in Christ. Those who mourned in that manner knew their loved ones died outside of God and Christ. They weren't born-again believers. They would have cried and mourned over this. Paul arrived in these cities and saw these things even among the saved people, and he knew it was wrong. He knew that those who died in Jesus Christ were free from the law of sin and death. The grave had no power over those who are bought by blood. Not just blood, but the blood of Jesus Christ. These will be brought back in the first resurrection and walk in radiant white with palm branches in their right hands into New Jerusalem. New Jerusalem here is a heavenly, righteous, and holy city created by God for God and His people.

In truth, it's not long now before Christ comes back for us. All these things will happen. If there are no such things, then our walk with Christ is vain. All the things we preach, teach, and profess are for nought. These things are just fables and nice fairy tales. But because we believe in Jesus' words and are convinced by the Holy Spirit, we testify to the truth. All the things written in the scriptures must be fulfilled. They aren't void words. They aren't words from a nice piece of ancient literature. No, they are the words spoken by God Himself.

Isaiah 55:11

"So shall my word be that goeth forth out of my mouth: it shall not return unto me void, but it shall accomplish that which I please, and it shall prosper in the thing whereto I sent it."

Here is a list of scriptures that tell us of the resurrection of the dead. And please note that there will be two resurrections. The first resurrection will be for those who have died in Christ Jesus. These are the ones who had a relationship with Jesus Christ. These are the ones who made themselves available to the call of Christ. These are those who made the case for Christ Jesus.

The other resurrection is for the damned. These are the folks who died as backsliders, non-repentant, atheists, and sinners in general. These people are raised to life for judgment and condemnation. These are the dead people John the prophet saw in Revelation 20:5, who were resurrected after 1,000 years. This is the millennial reign of Jesus Christ. When Christ comes again, the dead will be resurrected who died as born-again believers and will reign with him for 1,000 years, but those who died in sin will not be resurrected until 1,000 years have passed. To be caught up first with Christ means you are blessed and holy. It simply means you have no sin in your mortal body. You are perfect, sacred, and righteous before God.

1 Corinthians 15:12 Now if Christ be preached that he rose from the dead, how say some among you that there is no resurrection of the dead?

1 Corinthians 15:21 For since by man came death, by man came also the resurrection of the dead.

Acts 24:15 And have hope toward God, which they themselves also allow, that there shall be a resurrection of the dead, both of the just and unjust.

1 Corinthians 15:13 But if there be no resurrection of the dead, then is Christ not risen:

Philippians 3:11 If by any means I might attain unto the resurrection of the dead.

John 11:25 Jesus said unto her, I am the resurrection, and the life: he that believeth in me, though he were dead, yet shall he live:

Romans 1:4 And declared to be the Son of God with power, according to the spirit of holiness, by the resurrection from the dead:

Acts 17:32 And when they heard of the resurrection of the dead, some mocked: and others said, We will hear thee again of this matter.

Revelation 20:5 But the rest of the dead lived not again until the thousand years were finished. This is the first resurrection.

Hebrews 6:2 Of the doctrine of baptisms, and of laying on of hands, and of resurrection of the dead, and of eternal judgment.

Hebrews 11:35 Women received their dead raised to life again: and others were tortured, not accepting deliverance; that they might obtain a better resurrection:

John 5:29 And shall come forth; they that have done good, unto the resurrection of life; and they that have done evil, unto the resurrection of damnation.

Acts 23:6 But when Paul perceived that the one part were Sadducees, and the other Pharisees, he cried out in the council, Men and brethren, I am a Pharisee, the son of a Pharisee: of the hope and resurrection of the dead I am called in question.

1 Peter 1:3 Blessed be the God and Father of our Lord Jesus Christ, who, according to his abundant mercy hath begotten us again unto a lively hope by the resurrection of Jesus Christ from the dead,

Isaiah 26:19 Thy dead men shall live, together with my dead body shall they arise. Awake and sing, ye that dwell in dust: for thy dew is as the dew of herbs, and the earth shall cast out the dead.

He Is Not Here- He Is Risen As He Said

Matthew 28:6

"He is not here: for he is risen, as he said. Come, see the place where the Lord lay."

Death could not hold him captive because even in the grave, He is Lord. The story of the resurrection is documented in all four gospels. Each gives similar accounts of what had transpired. Jesus himself told his disciples that the Son of Man would suffer many things and then be glorified. This is the suffering of the innocent. He suffered for us, as Isaiah the prophet mentioned in his book of the same name, chapter 53. Christ needed to suffer the things prophesied of him. While we were yet sinners in due time Christ died for us (see Romans 5:6; 8). Christ died for the ungodly. Without Christ dying for us, we'd all be hopeless.

The Lord Jesus made a way for us when it seemed there was no way. This is the mystery of godliness. Godliness is different from ungodliness. Godliness is a complete state of being; however, the apostle Paul warned the young pastor Timothy that in the last days, people will have a form of godliness but will deny God's power (2 Timothy 3:5). Godliness used here to describe the people's condition is a type of religious affiliation and mindset. They know God's real, and he is to be praised, but they do the opposite. They can't go further than ten per cent, but they know God's aim is one hundred per cent. It's not ironic that the people who know God are the ones who disappoint him the most. The truth is that many people choose to follow religious beliefs, systems, and practices over God's love. They will say they love Jesus, but in works, they deny Him (see Titus 1:16). It's not what we say, but it's about what we do. If we say we love someone, we prove it. Love is an action word. Imagine we say we love God, but do nothing to prove it. We do this by pleasing God. We love everyone equally and do unto others as we'd like them to do to us. We don't pick out who we want to love and help. We don't only love our friends and those whom we have known for years. Some inside the church have had this mentality for years. They believe they're worshipping the Lord, but Jesus Christ knows the heart. Only if we perform the commandments of the Lord will we be serving him. As the Samuel prophet reminded King Saul: "To obey is better than sacrifice and to hearken than the fat of rams." This means that obeying God is better than doing things we think God wants. For example, we believe that if we keep all Ten Commandments, God will be pleased with us. In our minds, we may feel this way; however, no scripture states that if we do and follow the Ten Commandments, we'll be alright with God. The truth is, we need to understand the Bible. The lack of knowledge of God's word is destroying the people of the church. I don't believe in any denomination per se. I think that we all need to be holy to see the face of the living God. As Leviticus 11:44 states: "For I am the LORD your God: ye shall, therefore, sanctify yourselves, and ye shall be holy; for I am holy: neither shall ye defile yourselves with any manner of creeping thing that creepeth upon the earth."

In truth, I've studied many religions and church groups. If you tell me what church you attend, I'd know something about it. If you tell me what religion you're from, I'd know something about it. The truth is, we can search the entire world and study all religions, and still be on our merry way to the lake of fire. God calls simple people to accomplish extraordinary things. It's like in the story of Gideon the judge. The angel met him and said, 'You mighty man of power (see Judges 6). Gideon wondered what he was talking about. After all, he was from the tribe of Manasseh. His family was the poorest in the entire tribe. After all, he was just threshing wheat. Why would God bother with him? The Bible tells us that God is attracted to those who are humble and those who fear him. You may not be a doctor, lawyer, judge, prime minister, or holder of a PHD but the Lord wants to accomplish great things in you and for you. God doesn't care if you have a degree from a college or university. God doesn't care if you have a million dollars in your bank account, if you wear a lovely dress, or if you wear a nice suit. People judge us by how we look and what we wear. In truth, people need years to know us, and they may never get to. God knows us from before we were conceived (see Jeremiah 1:5; 1 Samuel 16:7). While others look at our physical appearances, God watches our hearts.

Jesus rose from the dead just as He said He would. On the first day of the week, Mary and the other women went to visit the tomb and found that the giant rock was rolled away, and they saw two young men who shone like the sun in white. They perceived it was angels. The truth is, we are seeking the living among the dead. We know Jesus rose from the dead. We don't need another gospel here.

Luke 24:5-8.

2And they found the stone rolled away from the sepulchre.

3And they entered in, and found not the body of the Lord Jesus.

4And it came to pass, as they were much perplexed thereabout, behold, two men stood by them in shining garments:

5And as they were afraid, and bowed down their faces to the earth, they said unto them, Why seek ye the living among the dead?

6He is not here, but is risen: remember how he spake unto you when he was yet in Galilee,

7Saying, The Son of man must be delivered into the hands of sinful men, and be crucified, and the third day rise again.

8And they remembered his words,

Remember, there's an order in the gospel. The first gospel that was preached, written, and taught to us is that Jesus died for our sins, was crucified, and was resurrected on the third day (see 1 Corinthians 15:1-6). Mary and the other women seek Jesus in the tomb because they thought he was gone for good. It's easy to doubt the words of God. Angels, on the other hand, don't doubt God's words. If we were to notice the angel's words, "Why seek the living among the dead?" They didn't go into long-winded storytelling about having faith or being of good cheer; instead, they told them it's futile to look into the tomb, since He has risen from the dead. It's just as the song has reminded us by Charles Price Jones: "Death Hath No Terrors"

Death hath no terrors for the blood-bought one,
O glory hallelujah to the Lamb!
The boasted vict'ry of the grave is gone,
O glory hallelujah to the Lamb!

Jesus rose from the dead,
Rose triumphantly as He said,
Snatched the vict'ry from the grave,
Rose again our souls to save-
O glory hallelujah to the Lamb!

The truth is, we too will ask Death a rhetorical question in the end: "O death, where is thy sting? "O grave, where is thy victory?" "The sting of death is sin, and the strength of sin is the law."(1 Corinthians 15:55-56)

Summary

He is not here! He has risen! We no longer need to look at his tomb because we'll find no corpse or bones. He's alive, and He's will.

To Believe or Not to Believe

To believe takes inward conviction. For one to think, he first must rule out all bias. He must empty his mind of what he was taught before and look at this message openly without prejudice. What benefit would there have been in writing a book like the Bible? The biblical theme includes, but is not limited to, sin, transgression, life, the resurrection of the dead, and related themes. Are these simply the imaginations of ancient peoples? Why doesn't the Bible talk about other things that would benefit our imaginations more? Why doesn't the Bible say that we'll be shipped off to some distant planet where there will be aliens enslaving us? If you had the opportunity to write a fictional story, you could write about anything, right? Now think about this aspect: if you got the chance to have written the Bible, what would you have included? Would you write that we were born as sinners and that we need to be free from sin? No, you'd have written that only if you're a theologian or someone obsessed with religion. But why's that nearly everyone who contributed a chapter or book in the Bible wrote of similar stuff? For example, why did Job write that there will be a resurrection of the dead? After all, Job wasn't a Jewish person or descendant of Israel? Job was likely from ancient Arabia. Some of these biblical authors weren't even in Israel. Many were in surrounding countries. For example, the Book of Jonah states that God called the prophet Jonah, who lived by the coast, to warn the people of Nineveh that, in forty days, the city would be destroyed. This is your typical book until a giant whale swallows the prophet and spends three days and three nights in its stomach.

Sceptics will tell you that this is another fictional story. But the truth is, what benefit would there have been to include the story of Jonah in the bible? Have we read any other stories of people swallowed by a whale who are praying inside its belly? And if Jonah is just a story inside the Bible to open our eyes to morality, why use such a story? The truth is, every book in the Bible is unique in some way. Many of these authors of the Bible didn't even live at the same time. Some lived 10 years apart to 1,000 years apart. If crazy men wrote all these things, we need to ask why mad people are obsessed with religion. Were Jesus and all these prophets and prophetesses crazy? Which author plagiarised another author's work? Surely, the only other person who quoted the story of Jonah was Jesus Christ. Why would Jesus and Jonah be obsessed with the story of a whale? Indeed, no other people seemed to be obsessed.

Sceptics say that the Bible was created to enslave the minds of its readers. But is this true? The only benefit the Bible could have played in this logic would be in terms of religion. Yet many people have read the

Bible and have tossed the book in the fire. The Bible has been distributed throughout all continents and in all languages, and yet many people are still wicked. People today are still free to choose who they want to worship in many parts of the world. Worship comes from the heart and not by force. The truth is that Christianity was practised in Ethiopia long before it reached Europe and the New World. Sceptics think that the church of Jesus Christ was started in Europe by Caucasian people, but the truth is that it wasn't. Christianity was in the Middle East, India, and Africa hundreds of years before it came to Europe and other territories. This same book today, called the "Holy Bible", that you can burn and pass as a foot mat, was an illegal book. The Bible was considered a dangerous book under the Roman Empire. Christians under the Roman Empire were persecuted for their faith in Jesus Christ. Many were killed and put in chains just for professing they loved and believed in Jesus Christ, the Lord. This sounds silly, right? Why would people be placed in chains and be killed for their religion or religious beliefs? But the sad truth is that they were persecuted. And even after Christianity became the accepted religion of Rome and Europe, they conquered the New World and parts of Africa with it in a violent manner, not remembering that they, too, were enslaved and were oppressed. Under Emperor Constantine, false religion flourished. We know about the Inquisition brought about by the Roman Catholic Church against Jews and Muslims. Where was that true and undefiled religion? Did Jesus command them to kill Muslims and Jews, and other people in his name? Not! They did that because they wanted to create a name for themselves. Jesus didn't tell them to do anything, and they know the truth as well. This is what Jesus commanded us to do in Matthew 28:19 and 20: "And Jesus came and spake unto them, saying, All power is given unto me in heaven and in earth."

"Go ye therefore, and teach all nations, baptising them in the name of the Father, and of the Son, and of the Holy Ghost."

"Teaching them to observe all things whatsoever I have commanded you: and, lo, I am with you alway, even unto the end of the world. Amen."

This is what happens when you have a religion but no genuine relationship with God and Jesus Christ: you eventually get utterly confused in your spiritual life. Indeed, Jesus didn't call us to take over countries and kingdoms. Clearly, Jesus said his kingdom wasn't of this world. Jesus reminds us to set our minds and hearts on things above, not on the things of this earth. Our citizenship is in heaven. This isn't a book on the history of world religions or the history of Christianity. Instead, this is a book to encourage those who believe to remain steadfast in the doctrine of Christ. There are thousands of books clearly on world religions and other religious belief systems. There are many books on Christianity and aspects of religion. The truth is, they are profitable for secular learning, but what we need is an authentic relationship with Christ Jesus, the Lord of hosts.

Let us pray

Father, we thank you for your absolute blessings and support. We thank you for our lives and those who you have sent to help us in this life. We know you're God all by yourself. The unseen God who supports us and our efforts once they are righteous and in your will. We thank you for your unending mercies. We thank you and give you praise for the miracles you'll continue to do. We come to you in the name of Jesus Christ, the only name that can set us free in this world and the world to come. The only name that is named in heaven and on earth. We declare you're Lord of our lives. We declare you are the God of old, working salvation in the world. We declare you're the God of our country. We believe and know you're the God who spoke to the apostles and prophets, and us in this time through your Son Jesus. We believe that before our time is up on earth, you'd have allowed us to fulfil our calling and purpose. We know that through you, Lord Jesus, all things are possible. You're the one who said: "All things are possible to those who believe." We hold you true to your words, Lord God, because we believe they are life and truth. We know you can't tell a lie nor repent as people do.

We have already won the victory over the evil one and this world because we believe in your name. We know demons and Satan himself are under our feet because of your name. And we praise you for strengthening us with the weapons for spiritual warfare—the sword of the Spirit we use, which is your word, God, to pierce Satan himself. We also have the breastplate of righteousness, the belt of truth, and all others.

Deliver us from evil, and let us not be overcome by evil, but let us overcome evil with good. Lord Jesus, all these things we declare in your name. Amen and Amen.